The purpose of this study guide is to provide supplemental educational material. It is not intended as a substitute or replacement of ON THE ADVANTAGE AND DISADVANTAGE OF HISTORY FOR LIFE.

Published by SuperSummary, www.supersummary.com

ISBN – 9781692615703

For more information or to learn about our complete library of study guides, please visit http://www.supersummary.com

Please submit any comments, corrections, or questions to:
http://www.supersummary.com/support/

TABLE OF CONTENTS

Arthur Schopenhauer
Barthold Georg Niebuhr
David Hume
Demosthenes
Edward Gibbon
Friedrich Hölderlin
Georg Wilhelm Friedrich Hegel
Girolamo Savonarola
Johann Christoph Gottsched
Johann Wolfgang von Goethe
Karl Robert Edouard von Hartmann
Karl Wilhelm Ramler

Ludwig Van Beethoven

Written in 1874 as part of his second *Untimely Meditation*, Friedrich Nietzsche's *Vom Nutzen und Nachteil der Historie für das Leben* or *On the Advantage and Disadvantage of History for Life*, considers the proper functioning of history in service to human (and specifically German) life and culture.

At the outset of his essay, Nietzsche distinguishes between advantageous and disadvantageous historical awareness. The "historical fever" in Germany at the time of writing is a disease in the culture. In the essay, his intention is to explicate its symptoms and antidotes.

Nietzsche opens Chapter 1 by claiming that what distinguishes humans from animals is the burden of memory. He discredits Barthold Georg Niebuhr's theory of the utility of the superhistorical, the notion that modern man can assimilate history from an omniscient perspective and deploy its lessons. History is made blindly; thus, when most fully understood, it is "unhistorical." When history serves life, it is therefore unhistorical, Nietzsche argues.

Nietzsche proceeds to identify three different kinds of history: the monumental, the antiquarian, and the critical. A balance of all three is needed if history is to serve life. Monumental history runs the risk of mythologizing the past and can discourage monumental acts in the present. Antiquarian history similarly is so focused on conserving the past that the present suffers. Critical history breaks with the past but can become disorientated as a result.

Another disorientating influence on modern man is the overwhelming superfluity of knowledge. This is indigestible and creates a divide between form and content.

This division in turn can impair a culture from the full expression of its qualities. In Chapter 5, Nietzsche expounds five problems that the overemphasis on history inflicts on contemporary society. All of them revolve around the falseness generated by an excess of knowledge, which in turn weakens society.

Chapter 6 is a discussion of justice and discernment. Nietzsche urges the restitution of truth, which exceeds and can cause disruption to the ego. Talented historians are rare, because objectivity is difficult and hampered by the mores of one's age. Therefore, one should "set a great goal" to avoid wasting the present (43).

Chapter 7 takes up the theme of annihilating history, which kills the present with the "minutiae" of the past (45). Whereas great acts are always veiled by a certain "madness" (46), fixation on the details of the past leads to indifference and apathy.

Nietzsche proceeds to argue that the fatalism produced by the historical education is vestigial of Christian theology, which occupies a similar position in the culture. The reverence for history is a consequence of this link with religion, which was made via Hegelianism.

In the penultimate chapter of the essay, Nietzsche critiques the well-known ideas of Edouard von Hartmann. Hartmann's concept of a "world process" is a "joke" for Nietzsche, for whom great actions take place in "timeless simultaneity" (58).

Returning in the final chapter to his original premises, Nietzsche's prescription for the epidemic of historicism and its corrupting power on the youth is a return to the natural, by means of the unhistorical (forgetting) and superhistorical (eternal). This will offer hope and the ethical inspiration required for the foundation of a true culture.

Preface

Preface Summary

Opening with a citation from Goethe that advocates utility, Nietzsche's essay sets out an intention to discern between historical awareness that aids life and that which abets it. Whilst asserting "certainly we need history" (12), Nietzsche says that his discussion of it will also seek to offer "public instruction and correction about our age" (13). Nietzsche says that his contemporaries in Germany were "justifiably proud" of the country's strong "historical education" (13). Yet this "historical fever" also threatens "decay." Nietzsche contextualizes his age and work within the pantheon of great civilizations, referencing the Greeks in this capacity. Finally, he expresses a hope that his work will "have an effect on the age to the advantage […] of a coming age" (13).

Preface Analysis

Providing context for his essay on history, Nietzsche defines his position within the canon: "my profession as a classical philologist" (13). His awareness of himself operating both within and against a tradition and an age thus provides both the form and the content of this essay. In Chapter 4, Nietzsche will argue against the division of these beneath the weight of what he deems an excessive historical education. This historicity impedes the course of meaningful action, a contemporary problem that he intends to both address and redress in this essay.

Chapter 1

Chapter 1 Summary

Look at a field of grazing cattle, Nietzsche writes. They are neither "melancholy nor bored" because they "immediately forget" (13). Humans remember, are aware that we will die, and are "encumbered" by this historical awareness. Happiness is "what binds the living to life" because it motivates us to live (14). Happiness is also contingent upon forgetting:

> "[…] whoever cannot settle on the threshold of the moment forgetful of the whole past, whoever is incapable of standing on a point like a goddess of victory without vertigo or fear, will never know what happiness is" (14).

Heraclitus's principle of constant flux, or becoming, is present in all action: "all acting requires forgetting" (15). The ability to instinctually forget and remember at the right time is integral to "cheerfulness, clear conscience, the carefree deed, faith in the future" (15). Nietzsche concludes "the unhistorical and the historical are equally necessary for the health of an individual, a people and a culture" (15).

The unhistorical is the foundation upon which what is correct and mighty grows. The moment of a great idea or great passion is typically experienced, Nietzsche argues, as a timeless "whirlpool." If it were possible to share this "unhistorical" perspective in the moment in which a great historical act took place, then this would be a superhistorical standpoint in the sense Barthold Georg Niebuhr uses the term.

However, it is not possible to hold such a perspective, because historical actions are taken blindly. According to Nietzsche, this is definitive: "Blindness and injustice in the soul of each agent [is] the condition of all activity" (18). If history is made in blindness, then history from the superhistorical standpoint is "dead." History in service to life is "unhistorical," and Nietzsche asks to what extent life requires the service of history.

Chapter 1 Analysis

In Chapter 1, Nietzsche establishes some of the premises of his argument and defines some of its key terms. One such term is the "superhistorical," which Nietzsche takes from Niebuhr, but not before discrediting Niebuhr's definition and appropriating the term for his own use. For example, take this facetious reading of Niebuhr, which implies that the omniscience with which contemporary historians claim to view history is impracticable: "[…] the superhistorical thinker illuminates all history of peoples and individuals from within, clairvoyantly guesses the original significance of the different hieroglyphs" (18).

The notion of the "unhistorical" is also important in the opening chapter, and Nietzsche uses it to further dismantle the notion of the superhistorical propounded by Niebuhr. In contrast with Niebuhr's omniscient superhistorical, Nietzsche asserts that the great moments of history occur in blindness. Thus, even from a superhistorical perspective, or the most illuminating investigation, they remain essentially "dead." In opposition to the prevailing investment of contemporary society in the social utility of historical education, Nietzsche claims that the fullest understanding of history is an awareness of the particular kind of blindness involved in its making.

Nietzsche calls the ability to forget in a moment of action the "plastic power" of a human being. Like Heraclitan flux, this plasticity is figured as transformative and potentially regenerative, "assimilating everything past and alien, to heal wounds" (15). If history is fixed because it is past, then the unhistorical is mutable. Nietzsche will elaborate on the significance of this "plastic power" in the later chapters of the essay, in which he discusses the uses of history in service to life.

Chapter 2

Chapter 2 Summary

Nietzsche re-asserts the importance of history in service to life. He distinguishes three kinds of history: monumental, antiquarian, and critical. Castigating "idlers," Nietzsche claims that the active human "uses history as a means against resignation" (15). Such individuals are motivated to increase the happiness of themselves, their people, or of mankind.

The monumental form of history is envisioned as a "chain" of individuals whose acts are "linked throughout the millennia" (15). In this kind of history, great acts are eternal. This is problematic because while such great acts may be inspiring, they invalidate lowlier lives. Nietzsche also disputes whether a great act may be extricated from its context. National, religious, and military days of remembrance fall into this category. Monumental history also runs the risk of mythologizing the past. References to the monumental acts of the past can also discourage new monumental acts in the present.

Each of the three kinds of history is appropriate only in certain circumstances. The antiquarian approach to history

assists a conservative approach, while the oppressed use
recourse to critical history to oppose their present
constraints.

Chapter 2 Analysis

Nietzsche's distinction between the three forms of history
he defines in Chapter 2 moves his argument forward by re-
classifying the contemporary notion of history. Defining
these three forms of history helps Nietzsche in his project
of dismantling history as a universal and unassailable
source of truth and wisdom. This fragmentation of the
concept of history serves to weaken it, since Nietzsche is
then more able to discredit each of the strains in isolation.

To a large extent, however, the kind of history to which
Nietzsche continually returns in this essay is the
monumental kind. He does so by contextualizing his essay
in the tradition that includes ancient Greek civilization at
the opening and close of the essay. The memorable
metaphor of giants calling to each other across the ages in
Chapter 9, and his appeal to art and religion in the same
chapter, also pertain to monumental history. It is this
monumental kind of history that is ultimately of greatest
service to human life, and with which he hopes to inspire
and unite the German youth of his day.

Nietzsche is concerned with the eminent moments of
history. Yet in seeking to insert his text into its pages, he
also shows awareness of what he calls "critical history." He
uses what he deems the failings of his own time as a
platform on which to erect his contribution. By navigating
between the different modes of historicism in his essay,
Nietzsche is also better able to move advantageously
between the roles of philologist, contemporary critic, and
historian.

Chapter 3

Chapter 3 Summary

In Chapter 3, Nietzsche turns to evaluate the antiquarian and critical forms of history. History, says Nietzsche, belongs to the "persevering and revering soul" who acts "in service to life" (20). The self experiences itself within the context of history. This elevates transient and humble conditions. Nietzsche likens the citizen to a tree deeply rooted in its history, and is against dislocating or uprooting populations.

However, the limitation of the antiquarian approach to history is a reduction in scope. This loss of perspective may in turn cause disorientation: "Here there is always one danger very near: [...] everything old and past [...] will simply be taken as equally venerable [...] while the new and growing will be rejected" (20-21). A second failing of the antiquarian approach is its undervaluation of what is in the process of becoming. This results from antiquarianism's overemphasis on preserving, rather than generating, life.

Nor is critical history without its problems. In severing the chain that links us with a history we consider unpalatable, we discover that our "new" history is less ingrained than our original one. Moreover, it's difficult to curtail this impulse to reject the past. However, on the plus side, critical historians will gain an additional nature, and can reflect that their original one was itself a second nature in an earlier time. Each of the forms of history have their proper place, each of which must be judged astutely.

Chapter 3 Analysis

In Chapter 3, Nietzsche moves from a discussion of monumental history to the antiquarian and critical. Nietzsche's central claim in his entire essay is rehearsed in miniature in Chapter 3. Here, he makes it clear that in his view, the culture suffers from an excess of the antiquarian kind of history, and his intention with this essay is to undertake a rebalancing of the role of history via a critical approach.

The role of the (German) youth whom Nietzsche discusses in Chapters 9 and 10 is clearly foreshadowed in his appraisal of critical history in Chapter 3. The notion of gaining an additional nature by uprooting the past is precisely the task that Nietzsche sets his "first generation": "the youth will suffer from the malady and the antidote at the same time" (68). This project is at the heart of his initial, stated ambition: "to have an effect on the age to the advantage" (12).

Chapter 4

Chapter 4 Summary

Having outlined the three forms of history, Nietzsche now concludes that every group of people must adopt an approach to history that is sometimes monumental, sometimes antiquarian, and sometimes critical, according to whichever history best serves life.

Nietzsche next turns to consider the modern humans' souls. The "modern soul" is distinguished for Nietzsche by a superfluity of knowledge. This preponderance of knowledge is "indigestible," thus producing a dichotomy between surface and depth in both the culture and the individual. A modern individual is contrasted with a Hellenistic one. The Greek would perceive modern culture as overly invested in historical education and encyclopedic.

The superfluity of information is also problematic because it produces an indiscriminateness that can lead to barbarism going undetected. For Nietzsche, modern culture takes place predominantly in the internal world; presumably by this he means the individual rather than the collective world. Nietzsche is critical of the disparity between content and form in the surrounding German culture. He argues that the lack of unity prevents the culture's full value from being made manifest. There is an urgent "need," Nietzsche claims, to rebuild the integrity between the inner and the outer in modern culture and life.

Chapter 4 Analysis

The preponderance of knowledge is a feature of modern life which has increased dramatically since Nietzsche's time, in what is called the "Information Age" of the internet, following the Technological Revolution. Some comparable issues are at stake today that stirred society at the time of the Industrial Revolution, circa this essay's publication date. Perhaps this makes Nietzsche's assertion that excess of information leads to division more intriguing. Too much information, according to Nietzsche, results in a division between the information itself and its packaging, which means that the "outside" is especially "barbaric" in contrast with the cultured interior. It is possible that the phenomenon of Fake News is an example of something comparable in contemporary culture.

In the context of the end of the Franco-Prussian War, it's hardly surprising that Nietzsche, after his long critique of German culture and manners, would advocate for "the unity of the German spirit and life after the annihilation of the opposition of form and content, of inwardness and convention" (32). In his effort to sew up the scattered fragments of Germany in this postwar landscape, Nietzsche looks to spiritual unity, which he says Germans "should strive for more ardently than political reunification" (32).

Chapter 5

Chapter 5 Summary

Nietzsche claims that the overabundance of history in an age is potentially damaging to its life in five respects, which he sets out in Chapter 5. Through excess, an age imagines itself as more worthy than other ages, or, alternately, as a latecomer, and thus regards itself with irony and cynicism. This paralyses society, which Nietzsche claims has grown lax and weak, its instinct blunted.

Individuals become unsure and lack self-belief in such an atmosphere. Outward identity, meanwhile, becomes a series of masks and puppets. Sincerity will redress this dichotomy between inner and outer, helping cultivate a society that responds to true need. Education, at present, too often serves to "teach [one] to lie to oneself about those needs and thus become a walking lie" (27).

The vacillations and cowardice of the modern soul are contrasted with the constancy of the Stoics. The contemporary ruling class could not be compared with the ancient Romans, since the former are "incarnate compendia." History is neuter according to Nietzsche, for whom neutrality pertains both to gender and objectivity. Criticism, the echo that an act has within the culture, is positive, because it means that the act has made an impact.

However, Nietzsche balances this remark with the observation that effusive criticism lacks potency.

Chapter 5 Analysis

In Chapter 5, Nietzsche continues his explication of the problems with excess history, developing on his assertion that the society of his time had a collective personality that had been "weakened." The chaotic inner world of society that was examined in Chapter 4 flows down into a discussion of how this affects the individual in Chapter 5.

Becoming an actor diminishes the value that individuals can offer society because they are engaged in replicating what has come before. The culture ceases to grow, in the sense that Nietzsche advocates in Chapter 10, where the "truth-in-need" flowers in parallel with the culture's ability to undertake Socrates' dictum, "know thyself." Nietzsche draws another example from antiquity, claiming that the fall of the Roman Empire was proceeded by a loss of cultural integrity; as Rome overreached itself, it "ceased to be Roman" (33).

In its appeal to the natural (substantially developed in Chapter 9), Nietzsche's thought may show the influence of German Romanticism, which, in 1876, was well established in the country. The movement looked to the perceived spiritual unity of medievalism as a source of unity for contemporary culture. The reification of the natural was typical of the Romantic frame of thought. For instance, Nietzsche's language is redolent with vocabulary pertaining to the Romantic register:

It appears almost impossible to elicit a strong full sound even with the mightiest sweep of the strings: it fades away immediately, and in the next moment it already echoes away strength less in historically subdued vapours. In moral language: you no longer succeed in holding fast the sublime, your deeds are sudden claps, not rolling thunder (33).

The sonorous notes of German Romantic composers such as Beethoven, Liszt, Wagner, Schubert, Schumann and Mendelssohn can almost be heard behind such hopeful passages of Nietzsche. Wagner is referenced on page 45, and Beethoven on pages 39 and 45.

Chapter 6

Chapter 6 Summary

Nietzsche now turns to interrogate the contemporary dictum that modern man is more just than earlier ages. Socrates claimed that to believe one has a virtue when one does not is almost insane, and more problematic than the shortcoming itself. Nietzsche praises the virtue of justice and discerns between ego-serving judgment and Last Judgment. Thus, Nietzsche distinguishes between truth, which has its root in justice, and "curiosity, flight from boredom, envy, vanity, play instinct–drives which have nothing at all to do with truth" (38). It is possible for equanimity, in inconsequential judgments, to mask an absence of "strict and great justice" in trickier verdicts; only strength can judge, and where weakness does so, it "makes an actress of justice" (39).

Nietzsche remarks that talented historians are rare, because many judge the past in accordance with prevailing contemporary ideology, and call this objectivity: "the work is to make the past fit the triviality of their time" (40). The term "objectivity" itself may be misleading for precisely this reason. Nor does art present a just picture of history.

Nietzsche is skeptical of the defensive claim that history is so complex as to be impenetrable: this is also not an objective position, but a subjective one.

Unlike scientists, Nietzsche argues, historians are at their least convincing when they generalize. History is better employed in elevating the "common" and "everyday" (41). This requires "a great artistic capacity, and creative overview, a loving immersion in the empirical data, a poetic elaboration of given types–this, to be sure, requires objectivity, but as a positive property." (41). Too often, the vanity of the historian leads to the conflation of unconcern with objectivity. It requires the greatest strength to interpret the past; otherwise, historians bring the past down to their level. The criteria for judging a historian is the quality of their generalizations, which will recast the familiar and draw profundity from simplicity: "History is written by the experienced and superior man [...] only a builder of the future has the right to judge the past" (43).

In conclusion, Nietzsche advises his reader to "set a great goal" in order to avoid wasting the present, and embrace "a hopeful striving" (43). This is in contrast with allowing the education of your age to exploit and control you. Finally, Nietzsche advocates fighting against the imperatives of one's own time: "become ripe and to flee from that paralyzing educational constraint of the age" (43).

Chapter 6 Analysis

In Chapter 6, Nietzsche elucidates the topic of discernment and justice in the context of his argument about the proper use of history. The chapter concludes with an appeal to the individual to exercise discernment and resist identifying as an *epigoni* (or follower). Once again, Nietzsche's aim is to recover the age from beneath the crushing weight of history.

In striving to set down the proper role of history, Nietzsche's close relation to post-Enlightenment thinking is clear. The comparison with science returns throughout the essay like a refrain. For instance, Nietzsche reckons with "the demand that history be a science" (28). Like scientists, he writes in Chapter 6, historians must be adept jurists of the truth. According to Nietzsche, the best historians are masterful artists with empirical data, steering a mean course between empiricism and aesthetics.

In his attempt to set history in its proper place, Nietzsche is both participating in and struggling against modernism. Awareness of historical context resulting in a loss of unity is a problem that Nietzsche addressed directly in the previous chapter, and one which is central to modernist thought.

Chapter 7

Chapter 7 Summary

Nietzsche perceives a danger in the historical sense which, if unchecked, can lead to the annihilation of life in the present. Creativity is discouraged in such an atmosphere, because the love and unconditional faith that are required for creation are inhibited by an overemphasis on the achievements of the past. This kind of history is destructive.

Christianity is, for Nietzsche, the example of this notion of annihilating history in action. Becoming unnatural and finally completely historical, the fascination of the church with "minutiae" is evidence for Nietzsche of its deterioration (45). While some contemporary theologians claim that there is a pure core to the religion, Nietzsche argues that the location of the true church is imprecise.

Nietzsche argues everything that is ripening needs "an enveloping madness, such as a protective and veiling cloud" (46). The atmosphere that surrounds the era is of indifference, "not to be excessively astonished by anything, finally to tolerate everything" (46). This, Nietzsche argues, is the consequence of a historical sensibility. If the youth are hastened ever faster to make scientific advances, they themselves will begin to degenerate, and the work will suffer. Scholars should think highly of the "people" for whom they write and are too often "practical pessimists" who lack hope for the future and thus live an "ironical existence" (48).

Chapter 7 Analysis

Interrogating another well-worn philosophical problem, Nietzsche now takes up the definition of the borders of the "true church." In the post-Enlightenment era in which Nietzsche famously proclaimed "God is dead," it falls to scholars and scientists, rather than clergymen, to distinguish good from bad, and the "ripe" from the "unripe." Thus, Nietzsche seeks to define the notoriously-ephemeral borders of the contemporary "true church" in Chapter 7. Nietzsche seems as if he would almost erect a Catholic rood screen between the present and the events of the past when he argues that the overemphasis on history threatens to rob the past of its mystery and "madness," and that an "atmosphere" is required for all great acts to occur.

The "veil" of madness that surrounds great acts is another typically Romantic idea. Through the application to a mythologized past, and to the mysteries of nature, the movement sought to rebalance the Enlightenment-era focus on the observable world through recourse to a more shadowy mirror. Romantic literature is full of obscurity, which is associated with greatness, profundity, and what is known as "the sublime" in Romantic discourse.

Chapter 8

Chapter 8 Summary

Drawing on a quotation from Goethe in which the writer and statesman says he has "an obscure inkling of his error," Nietzsche claims that the historical focus of contemporary education produces skepticism in "more highly developed historical men" (49). Nietzsche proceeds to argue that this focus on history is derived from Christian theological scholarship:

> Does not this paralyzing belief in an already withering mankind rather harbour the misunderstanding, inherited from the Middle Ages, of a Christian theological conception, the thought that the end of the world is near, of the fearfully expected judgment? (49).

Nietzsche is also critical of the notion that modernity is the culmination of history, because this apocalyptic mentality "is hostile toward all new planting" (49).

Furthermore, Nietzsche argues, judgment-orientated Christian theology has "dispersed itself into the skeptical consciousness" (50). This kind of history "makes its servants passive and retrospective" (50). Nietzsche goes as far as to state: "in this sense we still live in the Middle Ages and history is still a disguised theology" (50). Nietzsche turns to the idea of a "new age," arguing that such an era must neutralize the "problem" of history in establishing itself.

Next, Nietzsche shows the influence of Hegelian thought on the contemporary "idolatry of the factual" (51). Hegel's conceptualization of God, Nietzsche argues, privileges Hegel's own experience, implying that what follows is "redundant" (52). Nietzsche criticizes the passivity with which his contemporaries "bow" before history's power. There is an inconsistency in the conception that religion is extinct, ascribing a religious fervor to the modern preoccupation with history.

Chapter 8 Analysis

In Chapter 8, Nietzsche distinguishes between the "historical education" prevalent in his own time, and a truly "historical" individual, people, or epoch. The latter form of history is defined as being "strong, that is, in deeds and works" (48), which pertains to the "monumental" kind of history he has defined in the text's early chapters. Nietzsche likens the historical sensibility in Chapter 8 to a cultural "fever" (50). He advocates for the German people ceasing to students of an era of "fading antiquity" and embracing an unhistorical age, characterized by an "unspeakably rich" life. In the present historically-saturated culture, Nietzsche argues, modern people are "living memories."

In the contemporary deification of success, Nietzsche divines the influence of Hegelian philosophy, in which the idea, or "mind" is the ultimate. He calls this reification of the events of history "the tyranny of the actual" (54). The chapter closes by aligning forgetting and living, with the optimistic pronouncement that "there is a way of living which will erase this from memory" (54).

Chapter 9

Chapter 9 Summary

In Chapter 9, Nietzsche reiterates the position of modern man in relation to history: "Hard by the pride of modern man we find his irony about himself" (54). The awareness of history puts modern man in what Nietzsche calls an "evening mood," which verges on cynicism. This veering into cynicism is problematic because it limits opportunities for change and growth. Modern man, Nietzsche argues, posits human history as the evolution of natural history: "We are the apex of nature" (55). This knowledge, though, "does not complete nature but only kills [man's] own" (55).

Citing Edouard von Hartmann's *Philosophie des Unbewussten* (1869), Nietzsche claims that Hartmann's idea of the Unconscious is symptomatic of an excess of historical knowledge. Hartmann's appraisal of modernity in the light of doomsday is, for Nietzsche, a "parody" of history. It is typical of the antiquarian, conservative history Nietzsche outlined in Chapter 2.

Nietzsche interrogates Hartman's notion that the individual should surrender their personality to the "world process for the sake of its goal, the redemption of the world" (57). Nietzsche argues that Hartmann's idea of the "world process" is "to the detriment of existence and life" and hence proclaims it "a joke" (59). Rather, Nietzsche envisions history as a "bridge" across the Heraclitan stream of becoming, formed by its greatest contributors: "the goal of humanity cannot lie at the end but only in its highest specimens" (57).

The notion of life purpose is laughable, besides a death by exhaustion through striving for greatness. Success should not be measured in worldly terms, which greatness exceeds. Paradoxically, Christianity is successful in the world because of its doctrine that worldly success is of the devil. Worldly egoism is the drive behind historical movements. A modicum of egoism is helpful, or "prudent," as Nietzsche puts it, in guiding the "laboring strata" toward practicality and enterprise.

Nietzsche concludes the chapter by returning to the discussion of Hartmann's thought. Hartmann praises worldly labor and criticizes the elderly. In contrast, Nietzsche champions youth and asserts that historical aberrations are in fact used by society to shape the youth into worldly egotism. Nietzsche warns that an excess of history can rob the youth of its best traits: justice, selflessness, and love.

Chapter 9 Analysis

Chapter 9 is dedicated to rubbishing the theory of history put forth in Edouard von Hartmann's *Philosophie des Unbewussten* or *Philosophy of the Unconscious*. Hartmann is variously described as a "jester" (59), a "rogue of rogues" and a "mocking spirit" (59). The main tenet of Nietzsche's disagreement seems to be Hartmann's idea of a "world process," which for Nietzsche is emblematic of the era's overemphasis on history. In its place, Nietzsche inserts the Heraclitan principle of becoming: "the individuals who constitute a kind of bridge across the wild stream of becoming. These do not, as it were, continue a process but live in timeless simultaneity" (58).

This idea of simultaneity is central to Nietzsche's essay, which is in large part focused on redressing a lack of cultural integration in Germany. Simultaneity is also a distinctly modernist value. To attain this symphonic unity,

Nietzsche looks outside of time, appealing to a Socratic, dialectical approach to truth. At the crux of his essay is the Socratic dictum "know thyself," which Nietzsche quotes on the final page of his essay (69). As though picking from the Aristotelian unities of time, place, and action, Nietzsche's conception of the great acts of history has them transcend time, taking place in a quasi-Platonic realm beyond the world.

Chapter 10

Chapter 10 Summary

The final chapter opens with the metaphor of a ship docking after a long voyage. Nietzsche claims that he is guided by "youth" and feels impelled "to protest against the historical education of modern youth" (63). The youthful impulse toward poetry a century before Nietzsche was writing was in Nietzsche's opinion a flowering not since seen in Germany. In Nietzsche's Germany, by contrast, the youth are developed to "be useful as soon as possible" (64). Nietzsche asserts that the contemporary belief that "there is no other possibility at all than just our tiresome actuality" (65) is a problematic one.

Nietzsche expounds his position on the contemporary youth further by arguing that the era's weight of historical education "anaesthetizes and intoxicates" the youth by suppressing the natural. For Nietzsche, nature is the "sole mistress" (65). He chastises the educational system for producing a "crawling brood of botchers and babblers" (65). Faith in the education system is misplaced, nor would Plato's Republic have worked. Nietzsche's fellow Germans cannot have a true culture because they lack rootedness in nature, or truth: "first give me life and I will make you a culture from it!" (66).

Returning to the definitions with which he opened his essay, Nietzsche distinguishes once more between the unhistorical and the superhistorical. The former is the ability to forget, while the latter is the focus on the eternal. Superhistoricism is found in art and religion, which are opposed to science. This is because science relies on observation and the accretion of knowledge, which implies contingency. This is the opposite of the eternal, which Nietzsche poetically describes as: "an endless-unlimited light-wave-sea of known becoming" (67).

Nietzsche weighs knowledge against life and rates life higher, because knowledge is contained within life. The youth will suffer both the malady of excessive historicism and be supported by its antidotes: namely, the unhistorical and the superhistorical. Hope will inspire this comparatively uneducated youth, who will use the three kinds of history (monumental, antiquarian and critical) in service to life. This new generation will be indifferent to what is famous, and perhaps even to what is good, but they will have become human and hopeful again, Nietzsche claims.

Finally, Nietzsche reflects on the peoples of history, stating that the Greeks produced the truest and most regenerative culture because they observed the Delphic motto: "know thyself." It was the ethical strength of the Greeks that led to their "victory over all other cultures" (69). The essay concludes by stating that the fall of a prevailing, decorative culture may be justified by the advancement of a true culture.

Chapter 10 Analysis

In Chapter 10, Nietzsche asserts a need to establish a "first generation" of Germans who will produce a cultural flowering, unimpeded by the historical education that leads them to alienate themselves from their true nature. This notion contains the seed for Nietzsche's more famous theory, made infamous by its cooption by the Nazi Socialist Party some fifty years later, of the *Ubermensch*, or "ideal man. "First formally defined in *Zarathustra* (1883-85), the *Ubermensch* nonetheless raises his head in Chapter 9 of *On the Advantage and Disadvantage of History for Life*, in which the philosopher envisions the "giants" of different eras calling to each other "across the bleak intervals of ages […] undisturbed by the wantonly noisy dwarves who creep away beneath them" (58).

In this final chapter, which is concerned with the proper education of a society, Nietzsche refers to the ideas of the father of philosophy, Plato. Plato's famous theories about education, expounded in *The Republic*, are latently discernable in Nietzsche's final appraisal of the function of history for life and society. Adopting Plato's own notion of the *aeterna veritas*, or "eternal truth" of the "caste system," Nietzsche deposes Plato's "philosopher kings," claiming that "the Platonic state would have failed" (66). Evidently, Nietzsche considers his present society a failed version of Plato's envisaged Republic. It isn't long, however, before Nietzsche erects his own utopian Kallipolis, except that his is situated not on the Biblical rock, but in the abyss of modernism, the "endless-unlimited light-wave-sea of known becoming. If only he could live therein!" (67).

Arthur Schopenhauer

Nietzsche references Schopenhauer's *Samtliche Werke* on page 21, but the German philosopher is more famous for his treatise *The World as Will and Representation*. In this essay, Schopenhauer envisions the world as the product of blind metaphysical agency.

Barthold Georg Niebuhr

A German statesman, Niebuhr became Germany's foremost historian of ancient Rome. He inspired patriotism in his students at the University of Berlin through recourse to Roman governance. Nietzsche critiques Niebuhr's concept of the superhistorical (an omniscient understanding of history) in Chapter 1 in order to establish his own (the eternal) in Chapter 10.

David Hume

The British empiricist David Hume was an influential proponent of Enlightenment thought. He was also a historian, essayist, and economist. He is best known for his 1739 work *A Treatise of Human Nature*.

Demosthenes

Nietzsche mentions the Greek statesman and orator on page 61. Demosthenes's speeches were some of the most impactful of the 4th century BCE. His first judicial speeches were delivered at the age of 20, and he is an exemplar of the kind Nietzsche discusses in Chapters 6 and 10.

Edward Gibbon

Gibbon was a British historian and parliament member. Although on page 64 Nietzsche attributes the notion that "only time [...] is required for the world to perish" to Gibbon, this may be erroneous, as it does not appear in Gibbon's most famous work, *The Decline and Fall of the Roman Empire.*

Friedrich Hölderlin

The German philosopher and poet played a central role in German Romanticism, continuing the tradition of Goethe. On page 46, Nietzsche makes reference to a letter from Holderlinto Isaak von Sinclair, dated December 24, 1798. In the letter, Holderlin discusses the lives and works of the ancient Greek philosophers, in particular Diogenes Laertius.

Carl Heinrich Wilhelm Wackernagel

Alongside Jacob Grimm, Wackernagel was the most foremost Germanist of his time. Nietzsche cites him on pages 50 and 51 in his discussion of the German identity.

Georg Wilhelm Friedrich Hegel

Nietzsche writes that:

> [...] there has been no dangerous change or turn in the German education of this century which has not become more dangerous through the enormous influence, continuing to the present moment, of this philosophy, the Hegelian (52).

Nietzsche's grand statement refers to the German philosopher's influential role in German idealism, and Western philosophy more widely. His best known work, *The Phenomenology of Spirit*, is one of the most major modern additions to that canon.

Girolamo Savonarola

The Dominican preacher made a name for himself in Renaissance Florence by denouncing papal corruption and calling for reform. He is most famous for his bonfire of vanities, brief rule over Florence after its invasion by French forces, and excommunication. Nietzsche passes over this preacher in his discussion of Christian doctrine on page 50.

Johann Christoph Gottsched

The German literary critic was instrumental in bringing French aesthetic standards to German literature. His most famous work is *Versuch einer kritischen Dichtkunst für die Deutschen* (1730). He is mentioned by Nietzsche on page 64 in the course of a discussion of German culture.

Johann Wolfgang von Goethe

Goethe was a seminal writer and statesman whom Nietzsche cites continuously throughout his essay (pages 20, 24, 27, 35, 36, 44, 53, and 54). This wealth of references to the great German evidently show that Goethe is the sort of German who attained the kind of greatness about which Nietzsche is talking when he speaks of "giants" calling to each other across the ages, and a "first generation" of youths unimpeded by historicism. Nietzsche may have seen Goethe's Germany as a kind of golden age, before the battles that afflicted Nietzsche's own Germany with the division and dissatisfaction he describes. Goethe is an important figurehead in the essay, as both authority and emblem.

Karl Robert Edouard von Hartmann

Nietzsche calls Hartmann the "rogue of rogues" (57) and rubbishes the ideas set out in Hartmann's *Philosophie des Unbewussten* or, *Philosophy of the Unconscious* (published in Berlin in 1869) in Chapter 9. The German philosopher rose to prominence after gaining his PhD from the University of Rostock.

Karl Wilhelm Ramler

The German poet referenced disparagingly by Nietzsche on page 64 was a professor of logic at Berlin's military school before working as director of the national theater between 1790 and 1796.

Ludwig Van Beethoven

The German composer and pianist was instrumental in the shift from the Classical to Romantic schools of music. Nietzsche references Beethoven's third symphony, the *Eroica*, while describing the atmosphere of dissipation and lassitude caused by overreliance on history:

> "[…] the original note usually woke deeds, needs, terror, this one lulls us to sleep and turns us into soft men of pleasure; it is as though the heroic symphony had been arranged for two flutes and reserved for the use of dreamy opium smokers" (39).

Hegelian Philosophy

In one way, it's meaningless to say that Nietzsche's essay
has Hegelian influences, since Hegel sits over modern
thought and especially German philosophy in an almost
godlike role, a role that echoes in his own ideas. Nietzsche
writes that "[t]his history, understood in a Hegelian way,
has contemptuously been called the sojourn of God on
earth" (52).The influence of Hegel's concept of spirit or
"mind" is so profound it informed every aspect of the
Germany in which Nietzsche lived.

Hegel was a staunch supporter of the constitutional
monarchy of Prussia, the source of the contention and
discontent that in Nietzsche's view posed a hindrance to the
cultural integrity of the German people. It is almost
possible to replace the word "history" in the title of
Nietzsche's essay with "Hegel." At the risk of being
annihilated by the influence of Hegel, Nietzsche has to
carve some space between he and his philosophical father
by bypassing Hegel altogether and appealing directly to a
classical thinker of whom Hegel wrote: Heraclitus.

The Hegelianism of Nietzsche's essay is undeniable, and
the now-obscure contenders Nietzsche summons (like
Hartmann and Niebuhr) appear almost like stooges for
Nietzsche's contention with Hegel. The opening scuffle
with Niebuhr over the feasibility of a "superhistorical" (or
omniscient) perspective seems also to be a rebuttal of
Nietzsche's absolute idealism, or the notion that being is
comprehensible as an all-inclusive whole. Nietzsche's
argument for the incomprehensibility of history in the
moment of its making shows his awareness of Hegel. Or,
take Nietzsche's dispute with Hartmann over the latter's

concept of a "world process." The concept of "world process" is another inheritance from Hegel, whose philosophy places the emphasis on change, as opposed to stasis. Nietzsche's frustration with the reverence paid to history is echoed in his attitude to Hegelianism:

> I believe that there has been no dangerous change or turn in the German education of this century which has not become more dangerous through the enormous influence, continuing to the present moment, of this philosophy, the Hegelian (52).

Historians and the German Nation State

Nietzsche was writing in the wake of the Franco-Prussian War of 1870-71. His arguments about a culture in crisis and the contradictory relationship between history and politics must be read in this context. The freshly-formed nation was in a process of self-definition when Nietzsche was writing his tract about the function of history in 1874. The culture sought archetypal precedents in history to an extreme degree. Ramler and Wackernagel, whom Nietzsche mentions, were just the tip of the iceberg in a tidal wave of nationalist German historians.

Friedrich Dahlmann (1785-1860) was another such influential proponent of history whose retellings of the English and French revolutions paved the way for histories by Heinrich von Treitschke, Theodor Mommsen, and Heinrich von Sybel.

Dahlmann's student, Treitscheke, published *History of Germany in the Nineteenth Century* in 1879. The text mythologized the role of Prussia in reuniting the German nation state.

Mommsen made significant contributions to the *Monumenta Germaniae Historica,* a thorough catalogue of thoroughly-edited primary sources supporting the study of German history from the end of the Roman Empire through to 1500. Sybel wrote about German history in the Middle Ages, the French Revolution, and the German empire. Nor was Sybel without political interests. He sat on the 1850 Erfurt parliament, established a Historical Seminar in Munich with the patronage of King Maximilian II of Bavaria, and became secretary of the Historical Commission.

This saturation of historical study that concerns Nietzsche was objectively valid in one sense: despite the efforts of a multitude of scholars and politicians, history had still failed to unite the country in a shared identity. In one of best-known university lectures on politics, Treitschke stated "for many centuries it had been our tragedy that no one knew where Germany ends." Large sections of the population still opposed unification, holding fast to their nation-state identity. The question of the German nation looms very large in the background of Nietzsche's urgent call for a "truth-in-need."

Modernism

Many of Nietzsche's arguments rail against the modernity in which he found himself. Nietzsche's claim that life needs history directly opposes modernist theory, which is primarily concerned with emancipating modernity from outdated forms. Yet Nietzsche's reckoning with the proper role of history and the paradoxical relationship between history and life is a decidedly modernist project. The modernist agenda is especially palpably in the tussle in Chapter 6 about discernment, in which Nietzsche is especially mistrustful of there being a possibility of "objectivity." Writing history is difficult, Nietzsche says, because all things are couched in the prevailing ideologies of their time. It is this tussle, the very project of making new and "truth-in-need," which Nietzsche is at pains to advocate, with which modernism concerns itself.

Nietzsche's essay on the function of history is also modernist in its focus on temporality. The notion that history and civilization are inherently progressive came under fire from a range of modernists of the period. Schopenhauer's 1819 *The World as Will and Representation* called into question the optimism that had accompanied the Industrial Revolution. Charles Darwin's theory of evolution (*On the Origin of Species* was published in 1859) told a story about progress in the field of biology. Yet Karl Marx penned his equally-influential *Das Kapital* in 1867, shining a light on the contradictions inherent in capitalism. Nietzsche's essay is one of a series of meditations on subjective-versus clock-time, and the idea of recalibrating our relationship with time to reveal the essence of the modern.

Heraclitus and the Unhistorical

Central to Nietzsche's thinking about the proper function of history is his concept of the unhistorical. Defined in Chapter 1 against the notion of the superhistorical, or omniscient perspective, the unhistorical is the capacity to forget. The ability to "live unhistorically" is determined by the "plastic power" of the agent to discern between the helpful and unhelpful elements of the past.

Here and elsewhere, Nietzsche builds his notion of the unhistorical on the foundation of Heraclitus's classic theory of constant flux. For Heraclitus, as apparently for Nietzsche, life is flux, and to resist change is at odds with the nature of mankind. All that is great grows from the unhistorical. Nietzsche adds to the Heraclitan theory of the modernist emphasis on subjective experience. Developing on the Heraclitan idea of a river that can't be stepped in twice, Nietzsche describes the moment of inspiration or passionate love as a timeless "living whirlpool" of simultaneity:"he perceives at all he has never perceived so before, so tangibly near, coloured, full of sound and light as though he were apprehending it with all his senses at once" (16).

Imping his own theories so completely on classical ones is commensurate with Nietzsche's own notion of great, unhistorical actions. Nietzsche's unhistorical (whirlpool) differs from Heraclitus's flux (river) though in ascribing an additional sense of chaos to constant change. Nietzsche writes:

Every living thing needs to be surrounded by an atmosphere, a mysterious circle of mist: if one robs it of this veil, if one condemns a religion, an art, a genius to orbit as a star without an atmosphere: then one should not wonder about its rapidly becoming withered, hard and barren. That is just how it is with all things great indeed, 'which without some madness ne'er succeed' (45).

The addition of madness to Heraclitus's flux theory is critical to dismantling the historicism of Nietzsche's own time. Historical acts are made in "blindness" (18), so the surfeit of history in the present cannot be the path to greatness.

The Tragic

Nietzsche writes that "blindness and injustice in the soul of each agent [are] the condition of all activity" (17).If all actions are essentially blind, then the Nietzschean man is inherently tragic. Oedipally doomed to actout of blindness, madness, and chaos, Nietzsche's humans are tragedians, even at their zenith. Though man might strive for progress and attainment, as Nietzsche incites the youth to do in Chapter 10 of his diatribe on history, inherent in this hope is the "forgetting" at which his herd of cattle is so adept in Chapter 1. As "the apex of nature", it is man's burden to be aware of his own mortality, and yet unable to escape this destiny:

"[…] he is astonished that his memory so tirelessly runs in circles and is yet too weak and too tired to leap even once out of this circle. It is the most unjust condition in the world, narrow, ungrateful to the past, blind to dangers, deaf to warnings, a little living whirlpool in a dead sea of night and forgetting […]" (16).

Though the tragedy of mankind is inescapable for Nietzsche, it can be exacerbated by the stifling of growth, or the stultification that accompanies an overemphasis on history. This idea of repetition is intrinsic to Aristotle's famous definition of tragedy, "an imitation of an action." Acts therefore that repeat what have come before are for Nietzsche commensurate with the classical definition of tragedy. In Nietzsche's 1872 publication *The Birth of Tragedy*, Nietzsche embraces the primacy of the tragic mode in human life:

> A historical phenomenon clearly and completely understood and reduced to an intellectual phenomenon, is for him who has understood it dead: for in it he has understood the mania, the injustice, the blind passion, and in general the whole earthly darkened horizon of that phenomenon, and just in this he has understood its historical power (19).

IMPORTANT QUOTES

1. "I hate everything which merely instructs me without increasing or directly quickening my activity." (Preface, Page 7)

    It is with this citation from the influential German philosopher Goethe that Nietzsche begins his discourse on the value of history in its application to life. Goethe is symbolic of the kind of jurisprudence, action, and German-ness for which Nietzsche advocates in his diatribe on the role of history for life. In restoring the "truth-in-need" and natural impulses, Nietzsche sets out an ambition for his essay of invigorating or engendering new life in its readers, "quickening" them in the old sense of the word.

2. "Superfluous excess is the enemy of the necessary." (Preface, Page 7)

    Nietzsche is clear at the opening of his discourse that the value of history may be judged by its pertinence to life. He contextualizes his analysis in the contemporary German superfluity of historical education and scholarship. Nietzsche asserts that his role as a philologist is to critique the assumptions of his age in order to positively influence its growth.

3. "Man says 'I remember' and envies the animal which immediately forgets." (Preface, Page 8)

    Memory is used by Nietzsche to differentiate human beings from animals, and therefore is a defining characteristic of mankind. Humans, insofar as they remember, stand in opposition to nature, which is envisioned as a bucolic herd of cows in a field, and is

inherently "unhistorical." Since by Nietzsche's
reasoning memory prevents man from truly living in the
moment, and afflicts him or her with ruminations on the
past and awareness of mortality, history for Nietzsche
is intrinsic to the fundamental philosophical questions.

4. "[O]nly through the power to use the past for life and to
    refashion what has happened into history, does man
    become man." (Preface, Page 11)

    For Nietzsche, the capacity of mankind to negotiate
    both the historical (remembered) and unhistorical
    (imminent) is essential to its thriving. Nietzsche later
    elaborates on the difficulties of jurisprudence in
    Chapter 6, and argues that the ability to forget, or the
    unhistorical, is essential to any great act. This capacity
    to forget appropriately constitutes the "plastic power"
    of the human agent (67).

5. "The best deeds occur in such an exuberance of love
    that of this love, at least, they must be unworthy even if
    their value is otherwise immeasurably great." (Preface,
    Page 12)

    Nietzsche draws the example of falling in love (a
    "contra-historical" occurrence) to illustrate his point
    that both historical and unhistorical states are required
    in any successful action. The paradox, then, is that
    history is made of great acts, resulting from
    unhistorical motivations, or moments of forgetting.
    Thus, all actions are for Nietzsche inherently blind.

6. "History, conceived of as pure science and become
    sovereign, would constitute a kind of final closing out
    of the accounts of life for mankind." (Chapter 1, Page

14)

In his valuation of history only for its contribution to life, Nietzsche rejects the conception of history as comprehensible and instead isolates the value of history precisely in its unknowability. The "historical power" of an event is thus precisely located in its blindness and incomprehensibility. This notion of life as change dates back to Heraclitus and appears in the thought of major philosophers. Nietzsche's essay is distinguished by its project of reconciling history with the unhistorical.

7. "Fame is more than the most delicious morsel of our self love […] it is a protest against the change of generations and transitoriness." (Chapter 1, Page 16)

In contrast with Schopenhauer, Nietzsche defines fame as a continuity of epoch-defining acts. He envisions these monolithic moments as giants who call to each other "across the bleak intervals of ages [...] undisturbed by the wantonly noisy dwarves who creep beneath them" (58). Fame had a substantially different meaning for Nietzsche than it does for us today. It is figured in this essay as the reverberation of great acts through time.

8. "That this is the natural relation of an age, a culture, a people to history—brought on by hunger, regulated by the degree of need, held within limits by the inherent plastic power—that knowledge of the past is at all times desired only in the service of the future and the present." (Chapter 2, Page 23)

Nietzsche's conception of history is a plastic, or mutable one, which shifts in response to the prevailing societal need. Nietzsche's conception of power is the

*proper combination of historical and the unhistorical.
The combination of the two, of remembering and
forgetting, shapes great acts. This is the "plasticity"
that Nietzsche is talking about: the ability to change
and shape the course of history through well-judged
action.*

9. "The people that can be called cultured must in reality
   be a living unity and not fall apart so miserably into an
   inside and an outside, a content and a form." (Chapter
   3, Page 25)

   *In our internet-immersed age, Nietzsche's claim that
   prevalence of information can erode society's ability to
   discriminate is especially apposite. Nietzsche argues
   that only with integrity can true culture flower, and
   growth occur. His argument that the superfluity of
   information threatens the integrity of society is also
   especially relevant to the information age, in which
   society is facing new challenges to its sense of unity,
   and new kinds of confusion at its borders.*

10. "Modern man suffers from a weakened personality."
    (Chapter 3, Page 27)

    *Nietzsche argues that society has overindulged in
    knowledge and thus grown disaffected, complacent and
    diffuse. He uses the register of gluttonous consumption
    to figure society as a fattened gourmand: "a new
    stimulant for the weary palates; greedy for history"
    (27). More clueless than a child, he says, society has
    lost its instinct. A "strong" personality for Nietzsche
    appears to be one with the ability to defy the mores of
    the moment, and judge with discernment.*

11. "Only through this sincerity will the distress, the inner misery of modern man reach the light of day and the timidly hidden convention and masquerade can then be replaced by art and religion as true helpers, together to plant a culture which is adequate to true needs and not, like contemporary general education, only teach to lie to oneself about these needs and thus to become a walking lie." (Chapter 5, Page 34)

The insincerity of modern society is problematic for Nietzsche. He figures the contemporary society as artificial, and out of step with nature. Nietzsche's "walking lie" here clearly informed another seminal modernist text, Henri Bergson's An Essay on the Meaning of the Comic *(1900), in which Bergson describes the essence of the comic as rigidity and repetition, and in opposition to life's perpetual movement.*

12. "[…] only strong personalities can endure history; the weak are completely extinguished by it." (Chapter 5, Page 35)

The reason Nietzsche gives for this bold statement in Chapter 5 is that the individual who does not trust themselves will look outward to history for validation and understanding and become an actor. This statement is closely tied with Important Quote #10, which together form the crux of Nietzsche's argument against history. It is also literally true that in Nietzsche's conception, those who are incapable of great acts will not attain fame and will be forgotten. The weak will be the "noisy dwarves" that separate the looming giants of history. In this sense the weak are not only unactualized but obstructive to great acts.

13. "[…] the most terrible sufferings have come upon man precisely from a drive to justice which lacks power of judgment." (Chapter 6, Page 38)

Nietzsche argues that not only is the pursuit of truth in its purity rare, but that corrupted, this same impulse is disastrous. He claims that it requires both will and power to judge correctly, along with a commitment to "pure knowledge, without consequences." This statement of Nietzsche's illuminates many of the greatest atrocities committed by mankind. For Nietzsche, judgment is not simply an ability but a power, which confers godlike status on the upright judge, who is able to transcend their ego.

14. "Only from the standpoint of the highest strength of the present may you interpret the past." (Chapter 6, Page 42)

Nietzsche argues that those who lack the objectivity of the artist and the power of the impartial judge should not set themselves above previous generations in a position of judgment. Much like the last guests arriving at a banquet desiring the best seats, he says, this position of judgment must be earned, and is not a right. This statement of Nietzsche's also critiques his contemporaries' fixation on historical awareness as a means of informing judgment in the present. Nietzsche inverts the situation, claiming that only the most just can read history accurately, and that rather than treating history as a source of justice, we should engage in a "hopeful striving" for greatness (38).

15. "Form an image for yourselves to which the future ought to correspond and forget the superstition that you are epigoni […] become ripe and flee from that

paralyzing educational constraint of our age, which sees its advantage in preventing your becoming ripe, in order to rule and exploit you unripe ones." (Chapter 7, Page 43)

Epigoni, or the followers and imitators of artists and philosophers, are the subject of numerous classical works, including Sophocles's tragedy by the same name. In the play, the epigoni *are the sons of Thebes's failed conquerors, who perpetuate the violence by replicating their fathers' actions. Maturity, therefore, in contrast to these senseless sons, is what is required of the modern man for Nietzsche. Ripeness is defined by freedom from paralysis and a stance antithetical to the doctrines of one's own age. Through challenging contemporary mores, the future is built by these "superior" (43) individuals.*

16. "Only with love, however, only surrounded by the shadow of the illusion of love, can man create, that is, only with an unconditional faith in something perfect and righteous. Each man who is forced no longer to love unconditionally has had the root of his strength cut off: he must wither, that is, become dishonest." (Chapter 7, Page 44)

Nietzsche argues that the historically-oriented judgment of the present hinders progress by hampering the illusion of the dream of progress from taking root. Creativity cannot survive in an atmosphere that is overly saturated with monumental or antiquarian history, to use Nietzsche's terms. This is somewhat paradoxical in relation to his comments in Chapter 6 about the superiority and maturity of the truly historical individual, who is here defined in terms more usually associated with innocence ("unconditional faith"). It is

clear here, as elsewhere in the essay, that Nietzsche is
striving to set forth a well-balanced argument.

17. "Does not this paralyzing belief in an already withering
    mankind rather harbor the misunderstanding, inherited
    from the Middle Ages, of a Christian theological
    conception, the thought that the end of the world is
    near, of the fearfully expected judgement?" (Chapter 8,
    Page 49)

    In Chapter 8, Nietzsche draws out the influence of
    Christian doctrine, via Hegel, on the historical
    emphasis of his era. Modernity may have been stripped
    of its focus on mainstream organized religion, but the
    religiosity remains, and has been transferred to history.
    This is his main critique of the emphatic historicity of
    his time and the stimulus for this essay. Nietzsche
    argues that "man is tied to the memento mori", and
    that this focus on the past is detrimental to the new.
    Memorialization was a prominent feature of literature
    and art as well as politics in the face of an inscrutable
    modernity.

18. "Or is it not selflessness when historical man permits
    himself to be drained to the point of becoming an
    objective looking glass? Is it not generosity to renounce
    all authority in heaven and on earth by worshiping
    authority as such in every authority?" (Chapter 8, Page
    52)

    In line with his famous statement 'God is dead", in this
    quotation Nietzsche espouses one of the key tenets of
    modernism: its atheism. While modern society might
    imagine itself as post-theological, Nietzsche claims, we
    have found new theologies in which we believe perhaps
    more unquestioningly. The wealth of scholarship on the

past has a petrifying effect on the present, which in its uncertainty clings to all forms of authority. This outward looking attitude is part of the weakness that Nietzsche is talking about when he discerns between weakness and strength in Important Quote#12.

19. "[…] history always inculcates: 'once upon a time,' the moral: 'you ought not' or 'you ought not to have.' So history becomes a compendium of actual immorality." (Chapter 8, Page 53)

One of the most surprising pronouncements in Nietzsche's essay is his attack on the prevailing tendency to deify the events of history. He argues that the loss of religion in the western world transferred religious feelings to history. History is figured here and in the previous citation as a despotic leader, to which a culture unwaveringly submits.

20. "Modern man, that great garden spider in the node of the world web." (Chapter 9, Page 55)

As though foreseeing the creation of the world wide web more than a hundred years after this essay was published, Nietzsche imagines modern man as a spider sitting at the center of a web of "gossamer threads" of knowledge. Yet this superfluity of knowledge entails the "fragmentation and fraying of all foundations" and a "dissolution into an ever flowing and becoming." The information age has only amplified the effects of excess information that troubled Nietzsche, and we still find ourselves at the center of this web of information. It is unclear in Nietzsche's metaphor whether man is imprisoned by his web, becoming ensnared in it like a fly, or whether the web of information is a useful hunting aid that enables and furthers life. Arguably, we are still in the same position today.

21. "[...] the so wittily invented inspirational font of the unconscious and glowing in an apocalyptic light [...]." (Chapter 9, Page 56)

Nietzsche further contextualizes the position of modern man by arguing that it is precisely this information overload which is the bedrock for the notion of the unconscious. We are familiar with the term today via Sigmund Freud, but Nietzsche here cites Hartmann's influential 1869 publication Philosophie des Unbewussten. *The accumulation of untapped knowledge creates by default an unconscious and prevents the full resources of either from being tapped. The formation of the unconscious also has the effect of splitting the individual and the society. The ominousness of the image is due to its invocation of a feeling of alienation. Nietzsche could not have predicted the alterity we now experience in the digital age, but the apocalyptic feeling engendered by a superfluity of information is still with us today.*

22. "The devil [...] is the real power in all historical power [...] let egoism be our God." (Chapter 9, Page 61)

Nietzsche brings his tirade against his emphatically-historical era home with this striking metaphor, which he anticipates will "ring quite painfully in the ears" of such an age. Rejecting the Enlightenment emphasis on the temporal and observable world, Nietzsche champions a more Early Modern concept of worldly vanity. Since great acts occur for Nietzsche in an "atmosphere" and a moment of forgetting and disorientation, history cannot be deified in the way that

his contemporaries would like. Marx's 1867
publication, Das Kapital, *similarly pointed out the*
inconsistencies in capitalism, which, Marx argues,
entails the exploitation of labor for profit.

23. "One knows after all what history is capable of, owing
to a certain preponderance one knows it only too well:
of uprooting the strongest instincts of youth: fire,
obstinacy, self-forgetting and love, of dampening the
heat of its sense of justice, of suppressing or repressing
its desire to ripen slowly with the counter-desire to be
done quickly, to be useful quickly, to be fruitful
quickly, of infecting honesty and boldness of feeling
with doubt; it is even capable of defrauding youth of its
fairest privilege, of its strength to plant within itself a
great thought with brimful confidence and to let it grow
out of itself into an even greater one." (Chapter 9, Pages
62-63)

It is to the youth that Nietzsche looks in this essay to
carry the torch of hope for the future, and whom he
hopes to defend from the crushing weight of excessive
history. The awareness of the great deeds of the past
oppresses new life. Education is for Nietzsche a form of
enslavement in the sense that the historical education
so prized in his era prohibited the growth of the culture
in gradual and faltering efforts. Nietzsche figures the
youth and German culture as a ripening acorn, which is
disregarded because it is not yet an oak tree (45).

24. "[…] it suffers, so far as we are principally concerned
here, from the historical malady. The excess of history
has attacked the plastic powers of life […] the
unhistorical and the superhistorical are the natural
antidotes to the stifling of life by history, to the
historical malady."(Chapter 10, Page 67)

*In this conclusive passage, Nietzsche returns to the
primary tools that he has identified in the course of the
essay to preserve life from the mortifying effect of too
much history: the unhistorical, or capacity to forget,
and the superhistorical, or the eternal. The first is
found in nature, and the second in art and religion.*

*Overreliance on history is a sickness, Nietzsche argues,
that plagues contemporary society. As though afflicting
life with rigor mortis, history has suppressed the
discriminatory abilities of society, its "plastic power"
to refashion the past for the purposes of the present.*

25. "If only he could live therein! As in an earthquake cities
    collapse and become deserted and man erects his house
    on volcanic ground only hastily and trembling with
    fear, so life itself collapses into itself and becomes
    feeble and discouraged when the concept-quake which
    science provokes takes from man the foundation of his
    security and calm, the belief in the enduring and
    eternal." (Chapter 10, Page 67)

*Nietzsche shows that recourse to historical information
is a natural response to the Enlightenment tradition of
treating only the observable world as though it were
reality. The rumbling of Aetna over Pompeii
(discovered a century earlier) is perhaps discernable in
this passage, which turned a society to stone overnight,
just as Nietzsche views history choking the life from his
own Germany. The Biblical parable of the wise man
who builds his house upon the rock is also reversed in
this citation, underlining Nietzsche's claims that
modernity requires some recourse to the eternal, if not
in the form of religion then of history. Like Troy in
ruins, the city of modernism is turbulent vortex, bathed
in "apocalyptic light."*

ESSAY TOPICS

1. Can it be claimed that Nietzsche's essay is a modernist text?

2. Give an appraisal of Nietzsche's essay on the role history in the light of the sociopolitical context in which it was written.

3. How does your contemporary context affect your reading of Nietzsche's essay?

4. In what ways is Nietzsche's essay a reaction against Enlightenment thought?

5. To what extent are you convinced of the efficacy of Nietzsche's antidotes to excessive history (the unhistorical and the superhistorical)?

6. Examine Nietzsche's essay in the light of German history of the 20th century.

7. Goethe is quoted repeatedly in Nietzsche's essay. What role does he play in Nietzsche's argument?

8. How is Nietzsche's essay on history useful for life today?

9. In what ways does Nietzsche contend with Hegelianism in this essay?

10. To what extent is Nietzsche successful in discrediting the idea of a "world process"?